Contents

Any words appearing in the text in bold, **like this**, are explained in the glossary. You can also look out for them in the Word bank at the bottom of each page.

Born to work

The records below from 1815 in Newbury Port, Massachusetts, United States, show how little factory workers were paid each week:

It is dark and freezing outside. You are shaken awake and told to get out of your warm bed. It is only 4 a.m. After dressing in a hurry, you start the long walk to work. If you arrive late, you will be beaten. Hard work starts at 5 a.m. with only a short break at midday. Then it's back to work until 10 p.m., followed by the long walk home. Your tired body aches as you fall into bed. The next thing you know, you're being woken up again . . . for yet another day of weary work.

Name	Age	Weekly wage
Dennis Rier		£2.77
Son, Michael	16	£1.11
Son, William	13	83p
Daughter, Mary	12	70p
Son Robert	10	46p

One small slip and these boys could hurt themselves badly on this machinery.

Word bank   **labour**   work done for payment

Round the clock

For many children through history, days were filled with long, back-breaking work for very little pay. The small amount of money that they earned was used to buy simple things like bread. There was not enough left to spend on leisure, even if they had the time. Fun, games, or days out were rare things for most young people years ago.

It was common throughout the 1800s in Europe and the United States for young people to work a 16-hour day with little chance to enjoy real leisure time. What little free time they had was spent very differently from the way we spend our free time today.

Even in those days, when things were much cheaper to buy than today, this money would not have gone very far.

Today we have a much wider choice of what to do in our spare time, and it's usually much more fun!

Find out later

What games did children play over 500 years ago?

Which child actor was the biggest box office star?

What scary child **labour** happened in total darkness?

wage   payment of money for work done

Early times

Ancient Egyptian writings reveal a common saying from thousands of years ago. They show that children had to work hard if they were to have food to eat:

"You shall work your body when you are young, as food only comes by the effort of your hands and feet."

For thousands of years, young people were treated like small adults and were made to work just as hard. They were often sent to work as soon as they could walk, doing simple jobs at first. As their bodies grew and became stronger the jobs they had to do became much harder.

Ancient Egypt

Even four-year-olds would work with their parents 4,000 years ago. For boys, that often meant farming jobs, while girls had to learn household chores. Life was hard, with food shortages and a lot of disease, so young people had to grow up quickly. They would often be married by their early teens. People in their forties were thought to be very old.

The messages Egyptians left behind can tell us a lot about work and play from that time. ••••⋮⟩

Word bank   **pharaoh**   ruler of ancient Egypt

Play

The Egyptians left behind many messages and pictures on the walls of their **tombs**. Some scenes tell us that children spent their time looking after pets such as dogs, kittens, ducks, and pigeons. They also helped to look after farm animals like goats and cows.

As in other times through history, the rich had more free time and more toys to play with than the poor. When the **pharaoh's** children died, their toys were buried with them. Rag dolls, balls carved from wood or leather, throwing sticks, and painted wooden dolls with moveable arms and legs are some of the toys that have been found in Egyptian tombs.

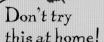

Don't try this at home!

One of the games Egyptian boys played was called "the kid is made to fall". Two boys would sit facing each other and would hold each other's hands. A third boy would try to jump over their arms. The idea was to catch the jumper's foot and make him fall. It could be painful!

This child-mummy of the ancient Nazca civilisation can be seen at Paracas National Park, Peru.

tomb   burial chamber for dead people

Greeks & Romans

Greek combat sport

Many young Greeks spent their leisure time boxing and wrestling. Wrestlers were not allowed to punch, but breaking each other's fingers was not against the rules! They fought naked, but were coated in olive oil. This made it difficult to grip an opponent, and they fell and slipped all over the place.

Over 2,000 years ago, the ancient Greeks used slaves to do much of their work. Rich young people would have had time for lessons, sport, and games because hard-working slaves did all their chores.

The ancient Greeks took sport seriously, and many rich boys would have trained hard to run in the Olympic Games. Many boys were horseracing jockeys, as they were lighter than adult men, which meant the horses could run much faster.

Poorer Greek boys and girls would have been kept busy gathering fuel, keeping animals, and weaving cloth. They would have to fetch water, fruit, and olives, and clean the house.

The Roman chariot race in the 1959 movie *Ben Hur* is one of the most thrilling in film history. ⋯⋰

Word bank **chariot** two-wheeled horse-drawn vehicle used in battle and in races in ancient cultures

Romans

As in Greece, it was far better to be a child in a rich Roman household, with slaves to do all the work. Rich boys got to play ball games and race **chariots**. In fact, watching chariot racing and **gladiator** fights was popular in Rome. Many chariot drivers were as young as twelve when they started racing. Few would have long careers, as chariot crashes were common and drivers were often killed.

Sport and games were also an important part of training for Roman and Greek soldiers. Many wealthy Romans and Greeks became soldiers because they had so much time to train by playing sport.

The Romans also used cutthroat razors, like this.

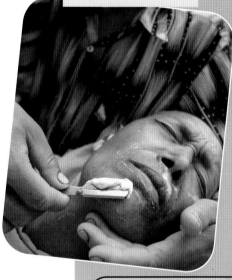

Footballers

The Roman lawyer, Cicero, wrote about some boys who got into trouble in their leisure time. They were sent to a court of law for kicking a ball from the street into a barber's shop. This startled the barber who was in the middle of shaving a customer. The razor slipped, he cut the man's throat, and killed him.

gladiator swordsman, or sometimes a slave, who fought for public entertainment in ancient Rome

9

Middle Ages

About 1,000 years ago, most people in Europe were **peasants** who struggled to survive. Only half of all people reached their twenties and few lived to be over forty. This time in history, from about AD 600 to 1500, is now called the Middle Ages.

From the age of about five years old, most children in the Middle Ages worked at home fetching water, herding geese, sheep or goats, or gathering fruit, nuts, and firewood. The Dutch artist Pieter Brueghel painted scenes of these peasant children in what is now known as the Netherlands. One painting, called *Young Folk at Play*, shows 24 different games that were often played in the 1500s. Many of them are still played by young people today.

Rolling the bones

Throughout history people have used dice for playing games. Dice games were very popular in Europe during the Middle Ages. Dried ankle bones of sheep were used for the dice, which were called knuckle-bones (below). To this day playing with dice is often known as "rolling the bones".

Word bank

banquet large feast for many people
falconry sport of hunting with hawks and falcons

Hawks

Across Europe in the Middle Ages, **hawks** and smaller birds, called falcons, were used by people to hunt other birds and rabbits. This was called **falconry**, and was a popular sport amongst the upper-classes in Europe. The wild animals caught by the hawks were often cooked for grand **banquets**.

Most young people living in big country houses would have kept and trained hawks. In England at this time it would have been common to see young people walking around towns and villages with hawks perched on their wrists, as they liked to show off the birds to passers by.

Rolling hoops

One of the most exciting games in the Middle Ages was racing hoops taken from old barrels (below). The idea was to use a stick to push the hoop to get it to roll. Touching the hoop with your hand was against the rules.

This is the famous Brueghel painting *Young Folk at Play*, from 1560. Which of the games do you recognise?

hawk   bird of prey with a hooked beak and sharp, curved claws

Marbles

For thousands of years young people have enjoyed rolling, racing, and flicking little balls across the floor. Early cave people played with small pebbles or balls of clay. Clay balls have been found in the **tombs** of Egypt, and in Native American burial grounds. Today's glass marbles started to be made by machine in 1902.

Early America

Some of the first Europeans to settle in North America arrived from England in the 1600s. They were called the **Pilgrims**. It was hard work for them to build their new homes, farm the land, and raise their children. Because life was so hard, many people died shortly after arriving.

Sunday was the only day when work stopped. It was a day for going to church, but not much else. Rules were very strict and children had to be quiet all day without being allowed to play at all. This day of rest was far from a fun or relaxing time. People sat in church for most of the day on hard wooden benches.

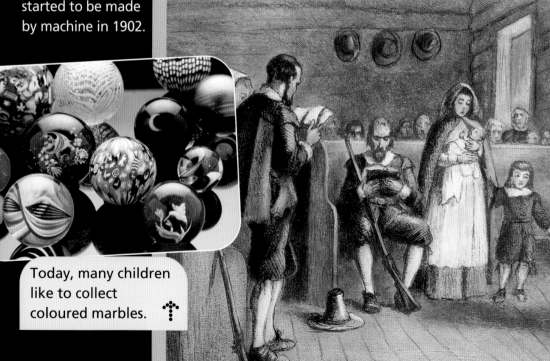

Today, many children like to collect coloured marbles.

Word bank **Pilgrims** first European settlers in North America

The outdoor life

Before the first Europeans arrived and settled in what is now the United States, Native Americans had lived there for thousands of years. In most Native American tribes boys helped the men hunt and fish; make bows, arrows, and knives; and carve canoes from trees. Girls would cook, make clothes from deerskin, weave mats, and make clay pots. There was always plenty to do.

Some Native Americans used the rounded tips of buffalo horns as marbles. They made small holes in the earth or ice, and gave each a score value. Then each player rolled the marbles down a slope into the holes to score. It was a bit like marble-golf!

Did you know?

Some Native American tribes, like the Cheyenne, played with hoops. They made wheels that looked like flat baskets. The game was to roll the wheels along the ground and throw spears at them. The score depended on where the spear hit the hoop. It was almost like aiming at a rolling dartboard. This kind of game would have been good hunting practice.

Sundays were for going to church.

Native Americans later played with hoops.

13

Young slaves

Selling children

Through history in different parts of the world, young people have been at risk of being kidnapped and sold as slaves. They could then be made to work without pay and beaten if they did not work hard enough. Slavery is officially banned all around the world today, but still goes on in some countries.

How would you like to be sold from one owner to another, and made to work as a slave? For thousands of years, both adults and children were bought and sold like this. In many countries slavery was once seen as an acceptable part of life.

Being owned

A slave is someone who is the property of another person. Although many slave owners cared for their slaves, others did not. Many slaves, both young and old, were beaten and starved. Even if they were treated well by kind owners, many slaves longed for the day when they could be free.

News stories still tell of criminals selling children into slavery.

14   Word bank   **bathhouse**   building containing many baths for public use

Ancient times

In ancient Greece and Rome, the families of soldiers who were captured in war were taken away as slaves. People who owed money and could not pay their bills would also have to become slaves, together with their children. If your parents were slaves, you would become one as well. In fact, parents who were free, but too poor to eat, had no choice but to sell their own children as slaves.

About 2,500 years ago, Athens, Greece, probably had more slaves than free people. Anyone who tried to escape was **branded**, or made to wear a collar with the words, "I have escaped. Send me back to my master."

Roman slaves

Roman slaves had to keep large fires burning for the Roman **bathhouses** and central heating systems. They would be expected to cook, clean, and do other household jobs. One Roman law said that if a slave killed his master, then all the other slaves in the area would instantly be put to death.

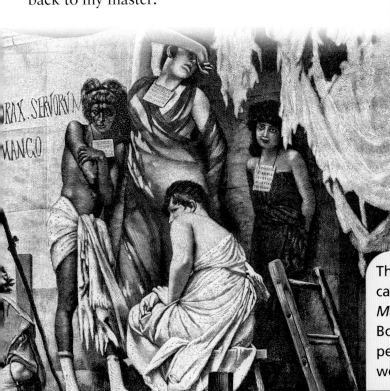

This is an engraving called *The Slave Market* by Gustave Boulanger. All the people with labels were sold as slaves. ❖•••

branded   marked by burning on the skin to show ownership

Two young African-American slaves.

African slaves

From the 1600s to the 1800s, rich slave-traders sailed to Africa and rounded up thousands of men, women, and children. They chained them up and shipped them off to the Americas to work on farms. The country needed more and more people to work in the large fields of cotton, tobacco, and sugar. Slaves were seen as the answer. Owning slaves, like owning cattle, showed how rich and important a farmer was. The more slaves he owned, the more crops he grew, and the richer he became.

Terrible punishments

"I was thirteen or fourteen years of age when I ran away to the woods. I was caught and put in Lancaster Jail, South Carolina, United States. I later made several attempts to escape, but was caught and got a severe **flogging** of 100 lashes each time."

– Adventures and Escape of Moses Roper, 1838

Word bank   flog   beat with a whip or strap as a punishment

Even young slaves had to work very hard, digging with a tool called a grub **hoe** to break up the hard ground. They left their huts early in the morning and worked until late at night. Sometimes they were forced to work all night long.

For life

Some slaves were able to earn a little money by doing extra work. They managed to save enough money over the years to buy their freedom. But they could only do this if their owners were willing to sell them.

Slavery dates

1782 to 1807
The United Kingdom sells over 1 million people as slaves around the world.

1833   The United Kingdom finally bans all slave trading.

1865   The United States finally bans slavery by law.

"When I was three years old, Mr. Brent, who owned me, moved to Virginia. My father, who was a free man, wanted to buy me and my mother out of slavery, but our master would not sell us."

– Thomas Johnson,
Twenty-Eight Years a Slave, 1909.

Many people who were shipped from Africa ended up living their whole lives as slaves.

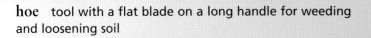

hoe   tool with a flat blade on a long handle for weeding and loosening soil

Industry

Against child labour

In 1832 one of the first groups in the United States to argue against child labour was the New England Association of Farmers, Mechanics, and Other Working Men. They said that, "children should not be allowed to work in factories from morning until night, without any time for healthy recreation."

Young people have always been used for cheap **labour**. In the 1800s heavy industry grew as the **Industrial Revolution** spread across the United Kingdom, United States, Canada, Japan, and Australia. More adults and their children were needed to work in mills, farms, factories, mines, and workshops.

Young people had to do a whole range of difficult and dangerous jobs. They worked at the bottom of dark, cramped coalmines and around huge machines in factories. Often young children were made to crawl into the machinery and fix things that adults could not get to. If they refused or failed in their tasks, they were often beaten.

The Crowd by Robert William Buss shows a chimney sweep on the streets of London. ⁘

Industrial Revolution   time of great change and development in industry and work

Up the chimney

The rise of coal mining during the new industrial age meant that coal fires heated more homes. The trouble with this was that their narrow chimneys often became blocked with soot. Large houses took on chimney sweeps to clean the blackened chimneys. The chimney sweeps were too big to climb inside the narrow chimneys, and so they used climbing boys to crawl inside and scrape the soot away. Many poor children got stuck inside, and some even died of **suffocation**. At the very least, they came out covered in dirty cuts and scrapes from the chimney walls.

If the climbing boys were too scared to climb higher, they would hear a shout from down below of, "I'll light a fire under you!"

Ending the misery

Sweeping chimneys was seen as a slave's job in the United States. Even though slaves no longer swept chimneys after 1865 when slavery ended, child labour went on for many more years. Chimney sweeps still used climbing boys until the early 1900s.

A climbing boy cleans the inside of a stove with his brush.

suffocation   when somebody dies through lack of oxygen

Throughout the
1800s in Europe
and the United
States, millions of
young people
worked on their
own family farms
or were hired out
to nearby farms
for very little pay
(below). If they
worked too slowly
to get the harvest
in before the rains
came, they could
be beaten. Long
hours, few breaks,
and not enough
food made their
lives a misery.

In the fields

By the late 1800s, in the United States, up to
2 million children under the age of fifteen
worked in farms, mines, and factories. As early
as 1798, cotton mill owners in New England
used children aged seven to twelve to work
around 12 hours a day. These children also
picked cotton out in the fields.

Working outside on a summer day may seem like
a pleasant job for young field-workers. But often
the work was difficult or dangerous. The weather
could be far too hot, freezing cold, or pouring
with rain. The work was often exhausting.

Word bank   **remote**   far away from towns and people

The need for change

It became more dangerous to work on farms as more heavy machinery was introduced. The children who worked on the machines were often involved in serious accidents. They could get **scalped** if their hair got caught up in moving parts, and hands and limbs were often crushed or cut off by moving blades.

By the late 1800s, many US states had passed several laws to limit the number of hours that children could work. Even so, in **remote** areas where there were hardly any police, the laws were difficult to uphold. By 1938, a new law was passed called the Fair **Labor** Standards Act. For the first time, minimum ages and maximum hours for different types of work were set down by law.

Today's farm danger

In the United States since 1936, about 36 percent of all deaths from farm accidents involved workers younger than twenty years old. This is according to a 2004 study done by the National Institute for Occupational Safety and Health. Even in the 21st century, about 300 children are killed each year in farm accidents across the United States.

These young farm workers could often be doing back-breaking work for up to 12 hours a day.

scalped   when skin and hair from the top of someone's head is torn off

21

Working in coal-mines could get very hot and stuffy. The work could be hot and sweaty, as most mining was done by hand. Miners often stripped off all their clothes to keep cooler in the cramped spaces. Low ceilings and dirty conditions made the work very tough.

Mules were used to pull coal buckets in some mines, as here in Indiana in 1908.

Down the pit

What could be worse than spending the whole day alone in the cold, damp, and dark underground? That was what life was like for young people who worked in coalmines in the 1800s.

Coalmines were scary places. They were pitch black, the tunnels were cramped, and the roofs were sometimes in danger of collapsing. The only light miners had was from candles or oil lamps. These would often go out. The flames were also a danger as there was always a risk of underground gases exploding.

Trappers

Many young miners were trappers. Coal was carried in huge buckets on underground tramlines. To allow the buckets to pass through the tunnel doors, a trapper would sit and open and close them all day. This was an important job as it helped to control the air flowing through the mine. It was meant to stop deadly gases building up in the tunnels. A trapper sometimes had to sit for hours in the darkness – alone, apart from the rats crawling all around the tunnel.

There were also all sorts of strange noises as the **roof props** groaned from the weight of the ground above. Sometimes there were rockfalls and clouds of choking dust.

Dirty air

All miners would breathe in black dust from the coal. The dusty air would get deep into their lungs. In later life many miners suffered all kinds of breathing problems because of their years of breathing black dust.

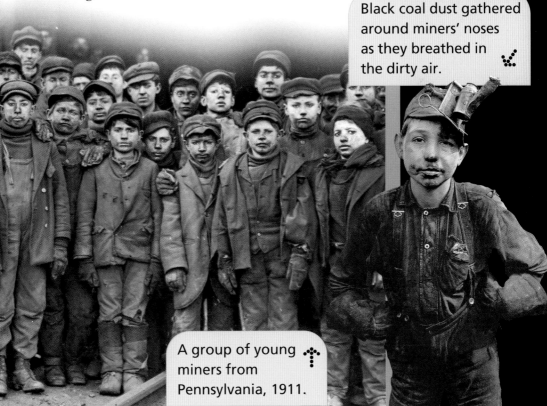

Black coal dust gathered around miners' noses as they breathed in the dirty air.

A group of young miners from Pennsylvania, 1911.

Even into the 1900s, many young people had to work hard in mills and factories. The picture below is from about 1908. It shows Furman Owens, aged twelve years old, at the Olympia Mill, Columbia, South Carolina, United States. He could not read but said, "I want to learn but can't when I work all the time."

In the factory

Throughout the 1800s many new factories were being built. These factories made glass, cloth, bricks, and iron for all the growing towns. More workers were needed to work in the new factories, and the cheaper the better! In the early 1800s about half of all factory workers in the northern parts of the United States were aged ten or younger. It was dangerous work for young people. They were so small that they had to climb on the machines to work them. Many would get their arms or legs trapped whilst climbing.

Weary and painful

Most young people had to work long hours in the 1800s. That could mean from 6 a.m. until after 8 p.m. at night. On top of that, there was often a long walk to and from the factory. Many workers were tired and worked slowly. They were often hit with a strap to make them work faster. In some factories, workers were dipped head first into a cold water tank if they were sleepy. Factory life was tough for everyone.

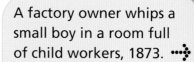

A factory owner whips a small boy in a room full of child workers, 1873. ⋯⋮

Here is a list of factory rules in the *Handbook to Lowell*, Massachusetts, United States, 1848:

- The bosses are to be always in their rooms at the starting of the mill, and not absent during working hours.

- The company will not **employ** anyone who does not go to Church on a Sunday.

- Anyone who shall take from the mills any yarn, cloth, or other article belonging to the company, will be considered guilty of stealing.

Yet another hard day's work for this young girl.

"Very often the children are woken at 4 a.m. The youngest are carried, asleep, on the backs of the older children to the mill where they work all day. They see no more of their parents until they go home at night and are sent to bed."

– Richard Oastler, interviewed in 1832. He led the Ten-Hour Movement, which tried to cut down children's working hours in the factories.

For just 57 pence, young workers in the early 1900s had to cut up fish all day. This often meant from 7 a.m. until midnight. Sharp knives, foul smells, and long hours made this very unpleasant work.

Work, pain, and pay

Young people had to work, or their families would starve. Some poor families had many children to feed. There was no sick pay, no free health service, and there were always bills to pay.

Some children would try to escape from factories, even though they needed the money. But bosses were ready with iron chains for anyone who tried to run away.

> "Even young women, if they tried to run away, had **irons** put on their ankles. These linked up to rings on the hips. They had to walk miles in these, to and from the mill where they worked."
>
> – from A Memoir of Robert Blincoe, 1828, by John Brown. Robert Blincoe was taken away to work in 1792, at the age of four, and died in 1860.

These young boys were fish cutters in Maine, United States. They were always cutting themselves.

World War 1

By the 1900s, more children than ever before were going to school. It was felt they should learn to read and write before starting work in their teens. Most teenagers in the United Kingdom and United States had to go out to part-time work. However, when World War 1 began in 1914, so many men went away to fight that young people had to fill their places in the factories.

In 1916 the United States passed a law to stop the selling of goods made by fouteen to sixteen year olds who worked over 8 hours a day.

In the movies

Charlie Chaplin was a silent-movie actor from the early 1900s. He made a film in 1921 called *The Kid* (below). It was a comedy, but it showed how tough life was for the poor. Jackie Coogan played "the kid" whose job was to smash windows so that Chaplin's character could get paid for mending them again! Find out more about Chaplin on page 45.

The girls take over in the factories during World War 1. ••••

Playtime

Cities kept growing in the 1800s as more and more factories and workers' houses were built. Many towns built theatres and music halls for entertaining workers in the evenings. Some of the shows and leisure events were put on especially for young people.

Showtime

In 1883 a special show called The Fays was held at Victoria Music Hall in Sunderland, United Kingdom. The advert called the show: "The greatest treat for children ever given." There were to be magic tricks, songs, puppets, and plenty of gifts and prizes. About 1,500 excited children went to see the show on a Saturday afternoon.

The Fays

Mr Fay toured schools and theatres in England in the 1800s with his fun magic show. He promised that every child who came would have a chance of getting a present. For just one penny, children could have a whole afternoon of fun!

Victoria Hall, Sunderland
On Saturday Afternoon at 3 o'clock
SCHOOL TICKET

THE FAYS

From the Tynemouth Aquarium
We will give a grand performance for children
THE GREATEST TREAT FOR CHILDREN EVER GIVEN
Conjuring, Talking Waxworks, Living Puppets,
The Great Ghost Illusion, and more

This tickets will admit any number of Children on payment of
ONE PENNY each; reserved seats 2d;
Nurses or Parents with Children 3d.

PRIZES :
Every Child entering the room will stand a chance of receiving
a present, book or toy.

This Entertainment has been witnessed by thousands of
delighted children throughout England.

The Victoria Music Hall, ···▸
Sunderland, where the
disaster took place in 1883.

Word bank   pantomime show for children, often based on a popular fairy tale

Tragedy unfolds

Up in the gallery, the young audience watched a clown on the stage as he shouted, "Come and get your presents!" Hundreds of excited children jumped out of their seats and ran down the stairs. However, the door at the foot of the stairs would not open wide enough for all the children to get through. They crowded into the stairwell and were crushed by all the other children pushing to get to the presents. Sadly, 183 children were trampled to death, and another 100 were badly hurt in the tragedy. Most of the **victims** were aged between seven and ten years old. Some families lost all of their children. What was meant to be a fun day out had turned into disaster.

Entertainment

Puppets, clowns, and **pantomimes** were popular with the young in the early 1900s, if they could afford to see them. Silent movies began in the 1900s. The *Keystone Cops* was a series of silent comic movies filmed between 1912 and 1917 that became very popular.

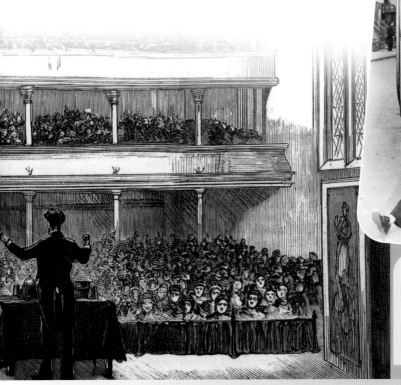

This is a funny scene from *The Cameraman*, one of the *Keystone Cops'* movies.

victim person cheated, fooled, harmed, or killed by another

29

Picnic disaster

About 100 years ago, it was rare for most people to travel very far away from their hometown. Passenger planes and family cars were unheard of, and holidays by train or ship were mainly for the rich.

However, in 1904, a church in New York planned a boat trip and picnic for a special Sunday school outing. More than 1,300 women and children eagerly walked onto the **paddle-wheel steamboat**, the *General Slocum*, for a day of fun on the East River. Sadly, the day ended in disaster.

> The *General Slocum* tragedy is one of the biggest disasters in US history. But it was quickly forgotten, and many people today have not even heard of the disaster.

Word bank   **paddle-wheel steamboat** boat powered by a large wheel with paddles around its edge

Tragedy on the water

Shortly after the steamboat set sail, smoke began to billow from the ship. A fire had started, and it began to sweep right through the boat. The crew panicked. They had not been trained to deal with a fire on board. The water hoses burst, and the wooden ship was soon ablaze.

The boat sped towards an island, but the extra wind fanned the flames making them higher. Few of the passengers knew how to swim. The lifejackets onboard were rotten, and the lifeboats were rusted to the ship. Over 1,000 passengers either burned to death or drowned. Their special day out ended in total tragedy. It is thought that the fire started with a spark, most likely from a carelessly tossed match, which had set fire to a barrel of straw.

LAST SURVIVOR OF *GENERAL SLOCUM* DISASTER, DIES AT 100 (2004)

Adella was a baby on the *General Slocum*. Her parents' clothes were on fire as they jumped with her into the river. Her two sisters were killed. Adella lived two years longer than Catherine Connelly, who was eleven years old when the *General Slocum* sank. Catherine never set foot on a boat again and died aged 109 in 2002.

Shirley Temple starring in the movie *The Little Colonel* with Bill Robinson.

Television

The last 75 years have seen major changes in leisure and entertainment. At the beginning of the 20th century, young people often had to travel a long way to enjoy a film, play, or show. But the idea of home entertainment started to develop quickly. The radio became popular during the 1930s. For the first time, families could gather around a radio to hear stories or plays in their own sitting rooms.

The next great breakthrough came when television was invented in 1928. It became more widely available to richer families across the United States from the 1940s. However, in 1945 fewer than 7,000 homes had TV sets in the United States. There were just nine TV stations. But this was soon to change as television became even more popular.

Great changes

More people could afford television sets in the 1950s and 1960s. Programmes were only shown for a few hours a day, all in black and white. Young people would rush home to watch programmes like *The Lone Ranger*, *Champion the Wonder Horse*, or *Lassie*. The most popular children's programme was *Sesame Street*, which arrived in 1969. *Sesame Street* has become one of the longest-running television shows in history, with well over 4,000 shows made. Life-like puppets entertain and teach millions of children in over 120 countries. The average weekly audience is about 7.5 million in the United States alone.

Years of television

Howdy Doody was one of the first programmes made just for children. It was broadcast live on the US television network NBC every Saturday, from 1947. Today, young people watch more television than ever before. By the time you are 70 years old, you might have spent 10 solid years just watching television!

The whole family sat down to listen to the radio (on the left of this picture) when it first became popular.

This is the puppet-character Howdy Doody.

33

Holiday fun

Over 150 years ago, hardly any families ever went on holiday. Any leisure time was a **luxury**, and few people could afford to go away. From the 1850s, when more railways were built, some families could get to the seaside for a week in the summer. Hotels were built in coastal towns and the seaside holiday started to become part of many families' lives.

In the United States there were lots of hot, exciting places to visit by the sea. In the United Kingdom, the weather was not always so kind. Sometimes families were to be seen huddled together on the beach, trying to enjoy themselves despite the wind and the rain!

Punch and Judy

Punch and Judy puppet shows have amused holiday crowds on UK beaches for over 100 years. Mr Punch has a hooked nose and a hunched back. He is very badly behaved towards his wife, Judy. The show still entertains audiences around the world (above).

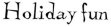

Word bank **boardwalk** walkway along a beach made of planks of wood

Atlantic City

In the 1850s one of the first US family holiday **resorts** was built. This was Atlantic City in New Jersey. Many workers from nearby cities began to visit this new town by the sea. The world's first **boardwalk** was built in Atlantic City, and there were soon huge amusement parks and nightclubs along the walkways.

In the 1920s the resort became known as the "playground of the rich and famous". The first Miss America beauty pageant was staged here in 1921, which brought even more crowds. The **seaside** leisure break became even more popular.

The world of Disney

Walt Disney opened Disneyland in Anaheim, California, United States, in 1955. 10 years later he bought land in Orlando, Florida, for other theme parks. Here, Walt Disney World opened to the public in 1971. The exciting rides and attractions include Magic Kingdom, EPCOT, Disney's MGM Studios, and Disney's Animal Kingdom.

Dressed for the beach in 1880, Rhode Island, United States.

Thousands of families from all around the world visit Disney World every year.

resort   place providing recreation and entertainment to holiday-makers

Games and toys

Toys have amused children of all ages for thousands of years. Yo-yos appear on old Egyptian wall paintings, and ancient Greeks made them out of clay. The modern yo-yo came from the Philippines, and today yo-yo competitions take place all over the world.

Rollerskates

Joseph Merlin lived in London in the mid-1700s. He replaced the blades on his ice skates with metal wheels. To show off his new rollerskates he swept into a party . . . and smashed straight into a mirror! One hundred years later, a rollerskating craze swept the United States and Europe. Rollerskates and rollerblades are very popular today.

Large-scale models are also made with Lego.

New toy

Over 100 years ago, only a few people owned a cuddly bear. The president of the United States at the time was Theodore Roosevelt, who was known as Teddy. In 1902 he went hunting in Mississippi. A story told how he refused to shoot a bear cub by saying, "Spare the bear!" A cartoon of this event appeared in a newspaper. That same month Morris and Rose Michtom, shopkeepers in Brooklyn, New York, displayed a soft bear, called "Teddy's Bear," in their shop window, next to a copy of the cartoon. Hundreds of people wanted to buy the bear-toy, and soon the United States went teddy bear mad! The Michtoms went on to make a fortune.

The Michtoms wrote a letter to President Roosevelt to ask if they could use his name for their bears.

Cabbage Patch Kids now come in many different characters.

Battles for a Cabbage Patch

Millions of dolls sell every year, often at high prices. The first Cabbage Patch Kids went on sale in 1983. These became the must-have doll of the year. However, there were not enough in the shops, and many parents ended up paying huge amounts for them. Some of the parents even started fights and riots in toy stores to get hold of the dolls for Christmas!

Up to date

For many people today, being young is far easier and more fun than at any time in history. The choice of games, entertainment, and toys has never been better. Young people in many countries now have more money to spend and more free time than ever before.

Unfair

It is a different story in poorer countries, and there is still cruel child **labour** in the 21st century. Long, hard work for little pay is still a problem for millions of young people. In some of today's poorer countries, almost 20 percent of five to fourteen year olds work for very low **wages**.

The Global March Against Child Labour, April 1998.

Word bank   **domestic**   relating to a household, family, or home

Child labour

Millions of young people today in parts of Asia, Africa, and South America have no choice but to work long hours if their parents have no money. In families where the parents die young from disease, the older children have to work to support younger brothers and sisters.

Young people in today's poorer countries work in mines, farming, **domestic** work, and making clothes or shoes, just as they did 200 years ago in Europe and the United States. Have any of your clothes or food been made by overworked, poorly paid people? If you knew, would it make a difference to what you buy?

Trade

Many young workers in poor countries work very hard to grow food such as grapes, bananas, pineapples, tea, coffee, and chocolate. But do they get paid a fair wage? If you want to make sure they do, you can check when you buy these foods. TransFair USA or Fair Trade are two organizations that work to make sure more of your money goes to the workers themselves.

Children in many countries still work long hours for little money. The boys shown here in 2003, work in a carpet shop in Multan, Pakistan. ⋯▶

Fair Trade has raised over £45 million in extra income for poorer farmers since 1998. ⋯▶

Guarantees a better deal for Third World Producers

FAIRTRADE

LUIS WANTS A FAIR PRICE FOR HIS CROP. THE FAIRTRADE MARK GUARANTEES IT.

CHECK OUT FAIRTRADE
www.fairtrade.org.uk

United Nations   organization of many countries, begun in 1945 to promote worldwide peace and security

Computer age

Some young people might find it hard to imagine life without PlayStations, Xboxes, DVDs, computer games, and mobile phones. Just a few years ago, young people didn't have any of these things to keep them amused. Was life duller then?

Some older people would argue that in their youth they used to make their own fun, were more active, and mixed with other young people more often. Other people argue that using computers can be good for the brain! The computer age gives today's young people more choice, but only for those who can afford such technology.

Mobile phones are the must-have fashion accessory of recent times.

Lucky children test out an early computer game.

Word bank   **graphics**   display of electronic pictures on a screen

Just calling...

As mobile phones get smaller, the people using them get younger! Mobile phones at one time were just used in emergencies. Now you can use them to play games, take videos, send text messages, and link to the Internet. They have become designer items for young people. In the United States, over half of all eleven to sixteen year olds now own their own phones. Toy companies are now marketing phones at much younger children.

Some doctors and scientists warn that mobile phones might be harmful, particularly for young children who have thinner skulls than adults. The radio waves they give out could be harmful to cells in the body. **Tumours** could grow in their brains or ears. Even the latest technology can have its risks.

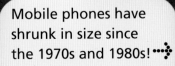

Mobile phones have shrunk in size since the 1970s and 1980s!

tumour   growth of unhealthy tissue in the body

The indoor life

On average, young Americans spend 38 hours a week doing indoor activities that require little exercise.

"Watching television, playing video games, listening to music, and surfing the Internet have become a full-time job for the typical US child."

– Dr Drew Altman, 1999, President of the Kaiser Family Foundation – an organization that works on health research.

Work and play, rich and poor

In the past, the way many young people spent their time was determined simply by the need to survive. When life was a struggle, the young had very few choices, chances, and rights. Today young people are usually protected by certain rights. In 1989 the **United Nations** agreed that every child should have the following basic rights:

• Enough food, clean water, and health care.
• A caring **environment** free from abuse.
• A good education.
• Leisure-time for play.

However, over 1 billion children today still do not enjoy these rights. Many of them have little choice about work or play.

More choice

Teenagers in today's richer countries now have many opportunities. They can usually work for fair **wages** in part-time jobs to pay for the wide range of entertainment and hobbies available. They can use the latest books and new technology to develop their education. After all, the chances for the young to learn have never been better.

A child from 100 years ago would be totally amazed at the choices on offer to today's young people. Surely no one today can complain of having too much lousy leisure or of being bored!

Some young people use their leisure time to work in the community. ⁘

Guess what?

Work does not have to be weary. What would be your ideal job? In a New York survey in 2005, over 1,000 thirteen to seventeen year olds were asked, "What kind of work would be your top 3 choices as a career?"

Can you guess their answers? Turn over to find out…

Find out more

Answer to page 43...

The Gallup Youth Survey of 2005 found the three top career choices of teenage boys and girls were:

1. teacher
2. doctor
3. lawyer

In 1977 boys put skilled worker at the top of the list, for example a carpenter, plumber, or electrician. The girls' top pick back then was a secretary.

Further reading

Issues of the World: Fair Trade?, Adrian Cooper (Stargazer, 2005)

The General Slocum Steamboat Fire of 1904, Ellen V. Libretto (Rosen, 2004)

Witness to History: Industrial Revolution, Sean Connolly (Heinemann Library, 2004)

Using the Internet

Explore the Internet to find out more about childhood work and leisure through time. You can use a search engine, such as **www.yahooligans.com**, and type in keywords such as:

- chimney sweeps
- Punch and Judy
- slavery

Search tips

There are so many pages on the Internet it can be difficult to find exactly what you are looking for.

These search tips will help you find useful websites more quickly:

- Know exactly what you want to find out about first.
- Use two to six keywords in a search, putting the most important words first.
- Be precise. Only use names of people, places, or things.

44

Hard times

"We went to the mill at 5 a.m. We worked until dinnertime and then to 9 or 10 p.m. On Saturday it could be until 11 and often until 12 p.m. We were sent to clean the machinery on Sunday."

– A man interviewed in the United Kingdom in 1849, who had worked in a mill as a child.

Charlie Chaplin and The Kid

The story of the movie *The Kid*, from 1921, drew from Charlie Chaplin's real-life experiences. Chaplin and his brother, Sydney, were sent to the **workhouse** at a young age:

"Although we were aware of the shame of going to the workhouse, both Sydney and I thought it adventurous. But on that sad day I did not realise what was happening until we actually entered the workhouse gate. Then it struck me; for there we were made to separate, Mother going in one direction to the women's ward and we in another to the children's."

Glossary

banquet large feast for many people

bathhouse building containing many baths for public use

boardwalk walkway made of planks along a beach

branded marked by burning on the skin to show ownership

chariot two-wheeled horse-drawn vehicle used in battle and in races in ancient cultures

domestic relating to a household, family, or home

employ give work to someone and pay them for it

environment surroundings we live in

falconry sport of hunting with hawks or falcons

flog beat with a whip or strap as a punishment

gladiator swordsman, or sometimes a slave, who fought for public entertainment in ancient Rome

graphics display of electronic pictures on a screen

hawk bird of prey with a hooked beak and sharp curved claws

hoe tool with a flat blade on a long handle for weeding and loosening soil

Industrial Revolution time of great change and development in industry and work

irons handcuffs or legcuffs made of iron

labour work done for payment

luxury something for pleasure or comfort but not always seen as necessary

paddle-wheel steamboat boat powered by a large wheel with paddles around its edge

pantomime show for children, often based on a popular fairy tale

peasant poor person or farm worker

pharaoh ruler of ancient Egypt

Pilgrims first European settlers in North America

remote far away from towns and people

resort place providing recreation and entertainment to holiday-makers

roof prop pole or beam used to support a roof

scalped when skin and hair from the top of someone's head is torn off

seaside place by the sea, especially a beach area or holiday resort

suffocation when somebody dies through lack of oxygen

tomb burial chamber for dead people

tumour growth of unhealthy tissue in the body

United Nations organization of many countries, begun in 1945 to promote worldwide peace, security, and economic development

victim person cheated, fooled, harmed, or killed by another

wage payment of money for work done

workhouse where poor people went when they had no money to live. They were clothed and fed, but men, women, and children were separated.

Index